EASY JAZZIN' ABOUT

fun pieces for piano/keyboard duet

PAMELA WEDGWOOD

(with special thanks to Fay Gregory)

CONTENTS

© 1996 by Faber Music Ltd
First Published in 1996 by Faber Music Ltd
3 Queen Square London WC1N 3AU
Music engraved by Chris Hinkins
Printed in England by Halstan & Co Ltd

ISBN 0 571 51661 0

FABER *ff* MUSIC

Still waters

SECONDO

Still waters

PRIMO (EASY PART)

'Le Shuttle' all change

SECONDO

'Le Shuttle' all change

PRIMO (EASY PART)

Hot potato

SECONDO

* Pause last time only.

Hot potato

PRIMO (EASY PART)

At a manageable speed! (♩ = c.120)

* Pause last time only.

Hoe-down

SECONDO

Hoe-down

PRIMO (EASY PART)

The Hit Man

SECONDO (EASY PART)

The Hit Man

PRIMO

Straight talking

SECONDO

Straight talking

PRIMO

Cutting edge

SECONDO (EASY PART)

Cutting edge

PRIMO

With a good solid beat (♩ = c.98)

Free and easy

SECONDO

Free and easy

PRIMO (EASY PART)

Road hog

SECONDO

Road hog

PRIMO (EASY PART)

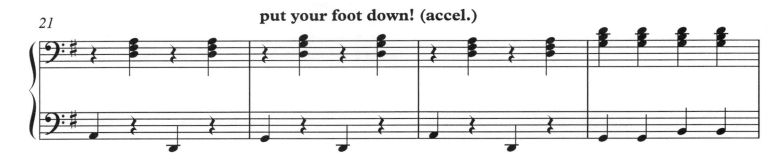

Canary walk

EASY PART

Canary walk